Royal
Horticultural
Society

RHS
Garden
Projects

Loads of fun things to make and do in the garden

A Dorling Kindersley Book

DK

LONDON, NEW YORK,
MELBOURNE, MUNICH, and DELHI

Senior designer Sonia Whillock-Moore
Senior editors Deborah Lock, Penny Smith, and Carrie Love
Designers Jessica Bentall, Gemma Fletcher, Rachael Grady,
Hedi Hunter, Rosie Levine, Sadie Thomas, Pamela Shiels,
Mary Sandberg, Gabriela Rosecka, Lauren Rosier
Additional editing Wendy Horobin, Lee Wilson,
Lorrie Mack, Holly Beaumont
Photographer Will Heap
Additional photography Craig Robertson
Food stylists Denise Smart and Annie Nichols
Picture researchers Rob Nunn
RHS consultant Simon Maughan
Food consultant Jill Bloomfield

Category publisher Mary Ling
Production editor Sean Daly, Clare McLean, and Tony Phipps
Production controllers Seyhan Esen and Claire Pearson
Jacket designer Rosie Levine

First published as in Great Britain in 2013
by Dorling Kindersley Limited, 80 Strand, London, WC2R 0RL

Material used in this book was previously published in:
Grow It, Eat It (2008)
RHS Ready Steady Grow (2010)
RHS How Does My Garden Grow (2011)

Copyright © 2012 Dorling Kindersley Limited A Penguin Company

2 4 6 8 10 9 7 5 3 1
191999 – 03/2013

A CIP catalogue record for this book
Is available from the British Library
ISBN 978-1-40932-494-2
Printed and bound by South China in China

Discover more at
www.dk.com

Contents

Sun symbol guide
What the lighting terms mean:

Full sun Partial sun Shade

For full sun, the plant needs 6 hours of direct sunlight each day. For partial sun, the plant needs 4-6 hours of direct sunlight each day. For shade, the plant needs very little direct sunlight, or none at all.

Soil-type symbols

Dry soil

Moist soil

Wet soil

Germination symbols

1 week   1-2 weeks

2-3 weeks   3-4 weeks

Introduction

This book is full of ideas of things you can do. The MAKE IT section shows you how to make labels and markers to use in your garden. It also demonstrates how to make a scare crow-like garden buddy, painted pots, dazzling decorations and creative containers.

Learn how to turn plants into food in the COOK IT section. Herbs become muffins, pumpkins are the main ingredient in pies, potatoes and carrots are turned into crisps, lemons are changed into ice lollies, and blueberries are used in the most delicious cheesecake.

Transform plants into brilliant projects in the CREATE IT section. Set up an enchanted path, a window box wildlife container, a wild-west cacti land, an ivy man, sweetcorn paper, and a container pond.

Families and children get inspired all year with RHS membership

Discovering new plants on the seasonal garden trails and participating in family fun activities are just a few of the many great days out enjoyed throughout the year with RHS membership. **Free entry** to the RHS Gardens is just one of several great reasons to join the RHS; you'll receive **personalised advice** and a **monthly magazine**.

For more information on joining the RHS and how you'll support our charitable work such as the Campaign for School Gardening visit **rhs.org.uk/join**

Make it

Cook it

Create it

Make It

7

What is a plant?

A plant is a living thing that feeds, grows, and produces new plants. There are nearly 400,000 different types of plant. They all have the same basic parts – leaves, stems, flowers, and roots.

Terminal bud
The main growing point of the plant.

Bees
and other insects help pollinate flowers.

Leaves

The leaves are where the plant captures energy from sunlight and uses it to turn nutrients into food. They are covered in tiny openings that let gases and moisture in and out of the plant.

Flowers

Many plants reproduce using flowers. Once the flowers have been fertilized, they produce seeds or fruit. Most non-flowering plants use their leaves, stems, or roots to make new plants.

Fruit

Stem

Stems support the leaves and flowers. They act as a transport network to take water, minerals, and food to all parts of the plant. They have growing points along their length that produce leaves and new shoots.

Roots

Roots anchor the plant to its surroundings. They also suck up water and nutrients that the plant needs to grow. Sometimes roots are used to store food and water.

Root hairs
These take up most of the water from the soil.

Root tip
This is the part of the root that grows.

How do plants grow?

Seed leaf

True leaf

Here we go!

Most flowering plants begin life as a seed. Seeds are little packets that contain everything a new plant needs to grow – the baby plant itself and food to get it started.

Seeds will only start to grow when the conditions are right. The seed takes in water, which makes it swell and split the seed case. The main root emerges and reaches down into the soil.

The seed then sends up one or two tiny leaves. These are called cotyledons, or seed leaves. These are quickly followed by the first true leaves. The seedling can now begin to make its own food.

Flowers – the inside story

Seeds form inside flowers. If you slice down through a flower you will see that at the base is a swollen chamber called the ovary. Leading to the ovary is a tube called the style, which has a sticky end called a stigma. Pollen is carried onto the stigma by the wind or insects. The pollen travels down the style to fertilize the ovules. The flower then falls off and the fruit starts to grow.

Flowers also use scent to attract pollinators.

Stigma

Style

Stamens
These produce pollen grains.

Ovary
This contains the ovules, which become the seeds.

Petals
are coloured to attract insects.

Labels and markers

Whenever you plant seeds, remember to make a label. When seedlings appear, it can get very confusing to identify which plant is which. Your labels can be as simple as lollipop sticks with names written on them, or you can have some fun making and decorating your own.

Some vegetables and fruits have many varieties and each one will be different. Look out for the variety on the seed packet and include it on your label.

Stone markers

Mark the pots that you have used with colourful stones. What eye-catching designs will you paint on?

Why not paint a stone in one colour and then choose another colour for a flower or the first letter of your name?

Paint

Tall labels

Labels on sticks will stand out in a pot. They are ideal markers for plants that will grow tall and bushy, such as herbs. Waterproof labels can be made using pizza bases, which are also easy to cut and paint.

You will need:

Recycle a pizza base

Kebab sticks

Re-use an old plastic bottle

1. Carefully cut off the base of your bottle.

2. Cut a small circle out of your pizza base.

3. Push your stick inside the circle and glue to the bottle base.

4. Now decorate your flower.

Basil

Butterfly

1. Draw a butterfly on a pizza base. Cut it out.

2. Push your stick inside the butterfly. Now it's ready to paint.

Lolly-stick labels

Lolly sticks are very handy as labels for small seed pots. Use pens to draw a picture of the vegetable you have planted or to make a stripy pattern in the same colours as the vegetable.

You can also use a clothes peg to label your seedling.

Paint the end of a lolly stick to measure how deep to make your seed hole.

1 cm (⅓ in)

2 cm (¾ in)

3 cm (1⅓ in)

Leek

More plant labels

Here are more ways you can help yourself remember what you plant. These jazzy plant labels will brighten up your garden. You can also make up your own designs using recycled bits and bobs from home.

Use old **buttons** to decorate your labels.

Flower power

Use an old **CD, plastic milk carton, pipe cleaner,** and **buttons** to make this dazzling label. Its shiny surface will also scare birds away. Stick everything together with a quick-setting, waterproof glue.

1. **Start by** cutting petal shapes out of the plastic carton. Stick them to the back of the CD, overlapping them slightly.

2. **Turn the CD over** and decorate with buttons and a pipe cleaner. Finish by attaching the flower to a bamboo stick.

Recycled **plastic spoons and forks** make perfect bodies and spike legs for these garden helpers.

Red lettuce

Pipe cleaners make good legs and antennae.

Sprinkle on **glitter** to add bling to your creations.

Plastic spoons and forks make great bodies.

Cut up **plastic cartons** to make wings and things. The plastic is soft and strong.

Plastic straws make bendy body parts, such as knees and elbows.

bubble wrap wings

plastic yogurt bottle

Garden helpers

Use washed pieces of packaging, such as **plastic cups,** and **foil food trays** to personalize your helpers.

Lettuce

Sage

13

Creative containers

Unusual containers for your plants will make your gardening projects interesting. Any object that has sides can be used, so keep a look out for possible ones to recycle and reuse.

When deciding what container would be best to use, think about the height and space the plants will need when they are fully grown.

Recycle food and drink containers.

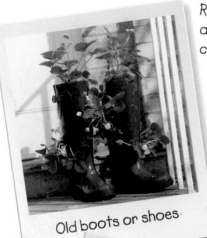

Old boots or shoes.

Use objects in a different way.

Wheelbarrow

Reuse old and broken objects.

Old buckets

Why not use old juice cartons?

14

Get ahead

If you can start early in the spring when the weather is still cold, get the seeds germinating indoors in these newspaper seed pots.

1 **Take a page** from a newspaper or comic. Fold over one long edge, twice. Roll the paper around a glass.

2 **Fold** the overlapping end of the tube inside the glass. This will become the base. Slide the paper off the glass.

3 **Looking** inside the tube, fold down the overlapping ends to make a base. Use the glass to flatten the base against a table.

4 **Fill the pot with soil** and then it is ready for sowing the seeds.

The newspaper pots will disintegrate when planted in the ground.

5 **Once the weather** is warmer outside, the seedlings can be planted in their newspaper pots straight into the soil, without disturbing the roots.

Get prepared

Whatever container you use, prepare it by following these steps:

1 **Ask an adult** to make some holes in the base to allow excess water to seep out. Use a liner with holes in if needed.

You could also use pieces of expanded polystyrene that small plants are bought in from garden centres.

2 **Put a layer** of gravel or broken pots in the base. This stops the soil from running out of the holes with the water.

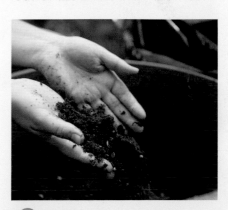

3 **Fill the container** with suitable compost. Most plants are happy with multipurpose compost, but others have specific requirements.

15

Make it

Seed-box organize

Many of the plants you grow in your garden produce seeds, which you can collect and then plant the following year. The secret of success is to collect the seeds at the right time and store them in the right way.

Sunflower seeds can be collected when the seed heads look big, fat, and brown. Cut off the whole seed head, put into a paper bag, and shake or pinch out the seeds.

Brilliant, bargain beans

Store seeds in a paper bag

1 Choose a healthy plant in your garden. Wait until the seed heads or seedpods have ripened and are about to split. Then, on a dry, windless day, cut off the entire seed head or pod.

2 Remove the seeds using your fingers. In a warm place, leave the seeds to dry on a piece of kitchen towel. Label and store the seeds in a dry, cool place until spring.

3 Prepare a pot ready for sowing your seeds. Some seeds that are very dried out may need soaking first to encourage them to swell and germinate.

4 Last year's seeds have become this year's new plant. Why not trade seeds with other gardeners and give some to your friends to have a go, too?

Onion seed heads   Lettuce run to seed   Fresh bean seeds   Corn flowers   Seeds scattering

Make a seed-box organizer

Your seeds need looking after while being stored, so what better way to keep them cool, dry, and safe than in your own seed box. If you organize them carefully, you'll know at a glance when to sow them next year.

SUMMER

Sun   SPRING

Runner beans

Courgette seeds

1 **Find a box** and a lid and wrap them in colourful paper. Cut out some season dividers from cardboard.

2 **Paint a colourful design** on the dividers. When dry, write SPRING SUMMER, and AUTUMN on them to show when to sow the seeds next year.

3 **Decorate small envelopes** using colourful paints. Also, you could draw or stick on your own plant pictures. Once the envelope is dry, put the seeds inside.

Dwarf french beans

Collected on 14th August 2012

Sow in spring

4 **Seal the envelopes** and label them with the name of the fruit or vegetable, its variety, and the date. Place in the organizer and cover with the lid.

Garden buddy

Plunder your recycling bin to create a wacky figure that will keep you company, and help keep birds away from your plants. Form his body from tin cans and lids, then add detail using plastic, card, or foil. When he's done, hang him from a tree, or tie him to a stake in the ground. Start by laying out all your junk and planning where each bit will go.

You will need:

Collection of junk

Garden wire

Wire from a coat hanger

Glue

Scissors

1 **Gather all your cans.** Ask an adult to make a hole in the base of each one by twisting in the point of one scissor blade until it punches through.

2 **For the arms and legs,** make a loop in one end of a length of garden wire and twist to secure. Thread the wire through one can, and leave the other end loose to connect to the body.

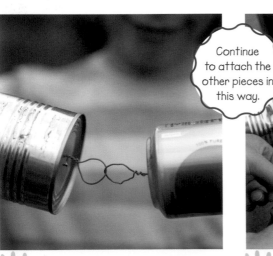

3 **To attach the next can,** loop a new piece of wire through the first loop before twisting to secure. Then thread this through the next can and make a loop at the other end.

Continue to attach the other pieces in this way.

4 **For the body,** make holes in opposite sides of a plastic bottle near the bottom. Insert a length of coat hanger wire through them, looping to secure at each end. The legs will hang from this.

Do the same to attach the arms higher up the body.

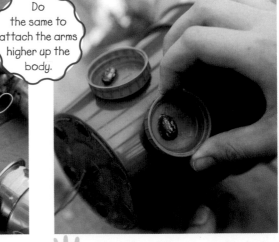

5 **For the figure's head,** use a plastic flowerpot, then glue on bottle caps for the eyes and nose. A strip of foil will make nice shiny teeth.

Top tip

CDs make shimmering
reflections that will
discourage hungry birds,
so tuck a few of
them inside your
figure's body.

String for hair

Foil for
hands

19

Painting pots

Decorate plastic or terracotta pots for your garden using acrylic paint, coloured markers, and glittery glue. Just make sure you give your pots time to dry before you fill them with compost and plants.

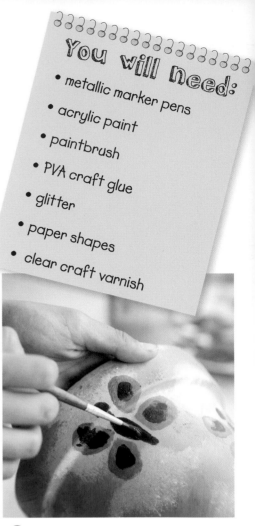

You will need:
- metallic marker pens
- acrylic paint
- paintbrush
- PVA craft glue
- glitter
- paper shapes
- clear craft varnish

Layer-painting a pot

1 **This method** is for a multi-layered picture. Brush a dark colour on the base of the pot and lighter shades towards the top.

2 **Wait for the first coat** to dry, then add another colour. We've dabbed on thick paint, straight from the tube, to make clouds.

3 **Add another layer** of paint when the second is dry. We have put butterflies on our pot, but you can add flowers, bugs, or whatever else you like!

Quick polka-dot pot

1 **Stick paper shapes** on your pot. We've used circles, but you can try stars or squares.

2 **Now paint over** the pot and paper circles with acrylic paint. Let it dry.

3 **Peel off** the circles to reveal your pattern. Either leave it plain, or paint the circles in different colours.

Use a silver metallic marker to make a magical night scene on a dark plastic pot.

Add a touch of luxury to a night time stroll scene using a **golden metallic marker.**

Try mixing **metallic markers** and **acrylic paint** to make a fiery pot for hot crops.

Paint bands of glue on your pot. Sprinkle them with **glitter.** Then repeat with another glittery colour.

Use the layer-painting techniques and make up your own designs.

for mum

4 **Turn your pot** into a present by adding a name.

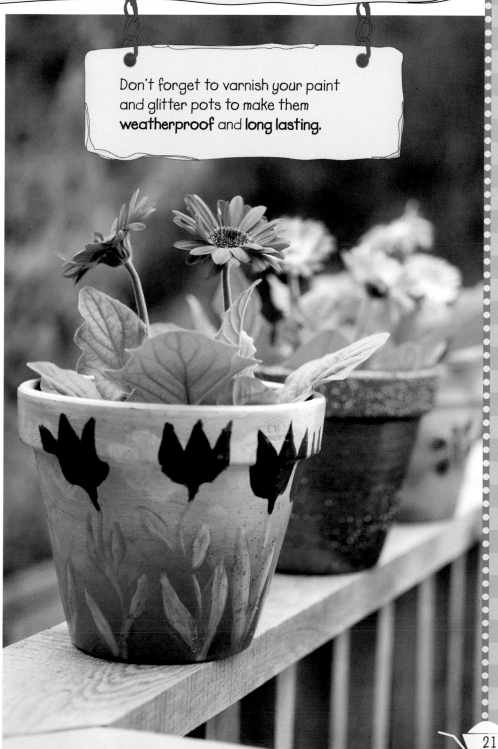

Don't forget to varnish your paint and glitter pots to make them **weatherproof** and **long lasting.**

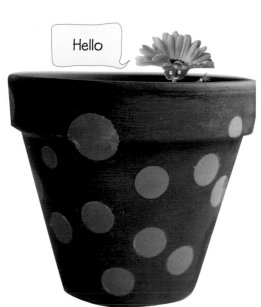

Hello

4 **The finished pot** – it's spot on!

Dazzling decorations

Colourful decorations poking up between your plants will not only add sparkle, but can also help to identify what you have planted, like a label. Try making a butterfly, flower, or bird. Alternatively, make up your own design that will suit your garden.

Flower

Bird

Butterfly

Did you know? Plants have two names: a scientific one often in Latin, and a common name, which may vary in different places.

1 Draw your design onto the base of a foil container, using a black marker pen.

2 Here are some ideas for your design. You could choose bugs, flowers, and birds.

3 Cut around the outline of your design using a sharp pair of scissors.

4 Press a pen onto the foil shape to make raised holes.

5 Colour your design with coloured permanent marker pens and let the ink dry.

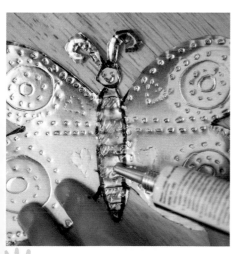

6 Spread some glue down the centre of your design where the stick will go.

7 Attach the stick and hold it on the glue until it is secure.

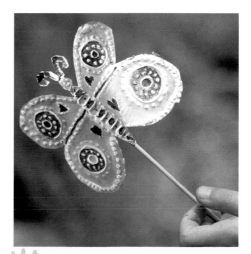

8 Find a place in your garden to put your colourful butterfly. Try putting it in a window box or flower pot.

Cook It

Herby cheese muffins

You will need:

- 280g (10oz) plain flour
- 1 tbsp baking powder
- 1 tsp salt
- 1 tsp mustard powder
- 125g (4¹/₂oz) mature Cheddar cheese, grated
- 2 tbsp chopped fresh parsley
- 1 tbsp chopped fresh oregano
- 2 tsp chopped fresh thyme
- freshly ground black pepper
- 2 eggs
- 200ml (7fl oz) semi-skimmed milk
- 75g (2¹/₂oz) butter, melted

Yummy

Here is a herby muffin recipe that uses parsley, oregano, and thyme from your garden. The muffins are irresistible and best eaten the day they're made, although they will last for a couple of days.

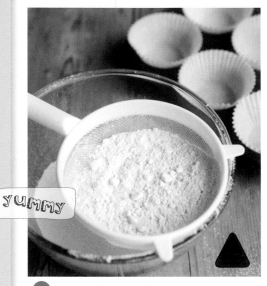

1 **Preheat the oven** to 190°C (375°F/Gas 5). Line a muffin tin with 10 paper muffin cases. Then sieve the flour, baking powder, and salt into a bowl.

2 **Add the mustard,** three quarters of the cheese, and the parsley, oregano, and thyme. Season with black pepper and mix everything together.

3 **In another bowl,** beat together the eggs, milk, and melted butter, and pour over the dry ingredients.

4 **Stir the mixture** until everything is just combined. Your batter should be quite lumpy.

5 **Spoon the batter** into the muffin cases, then sprinkle the rest of the cheese on top. Bake for 20–25 minutes until risen and firm.

Basil and tomato muffins
To make these, simply follow the main recipe, but swap the herbs for 2tbsp chopped fresh basil, and stir in 75g (2½oz) chopped sun-dried tomatoes.

You'll need

Mini pumpkin pies

Ask an adult to cut the pumpkin in half with a sharp knife, using a rocking motion. Scoop out the seeds. Slice the pumpkin into pieces, and cut off the skin.

peeled, deseeded
500g (18oz) pumpkin, cut into large chunks

1 tbsp olive oil

cut into 16 pieces
375g (15oz) puff pastry

1 tbsp plain flour

90g (3oz) treacle

1 whole egg

3 large egg yolks

300 ml (11fl oz) milk

½ a split vanilla pod

a pinch of salt

Pre-heat
190°C, 375°F. Gas 5

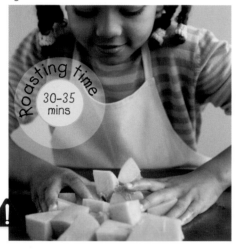

Roasting time
30-35 mins

1 On a baking tray, pour olive oil over the pumpkin pieces. Evenly coat them, using your hands. Roast until tender. Cool and then mash with a fork.

Refrigerate for 30 mins

2 Shape the puff pastry pieces into balls. Roll out each ball until about 6 cm (2½ in) diameter. Press each piece into a bun tin and put into the fridge.

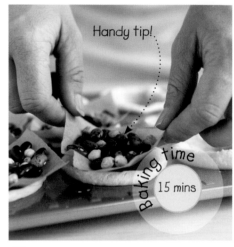

Handy tip!

Baking time
15 mins

3 Place a piece of parchment paper into each pastry and fill to the top with baking beans. Bake in the oven then remove the paper and beans.

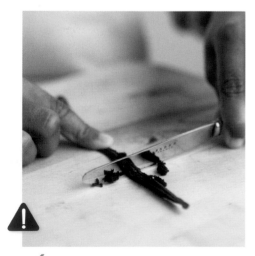

4 Pour the milk into a pan. Scrape out the vanilla seeds from the pod and add to the milk. Heat the mixture until just below boiling point. Leave to cool a little.

5 Lightly beat the egg yolks, whole egg, and treacle in a bowl. Add the flour and salt and beat until smooth. Strain the hot milk over the mixture and beat.

6 Pour the smooth mixture into a pan and bring to the boil, stirring all the time until thickened. Remove from heat and stir in the pumpkin puree.

7 Spoon out

the mixture evenly into the pastry cases. Bake in the oven for 20-25 minutes until just firm and slightly puffed up. Serve the pies warm with a dusting of icing sugar on the top if you wish.

Lemonade lollies

Keep cool on a hot summer's day with the zingy taste of your juicy lemons. Lemons add flavour to fish and salads as well.

Add slices of lemon to drinks and salads.

You'll need

18 lolly sticks

6 juicy lemons

250ml (8fl oz) runny honey

700ml (25fl oz) cold water

18 empty yoghurt pots

1 Finely grate the zest from three of the lemons and place in a pan with the honey and 500ml (18fl oz) water. Bring to the boil, then remove from heat.

2 Squeeze the juice from all of the lemons. Pour into a jug. This should give you about 200-250ml (7-8fl oz) of juice.

3 Strain the honey and lemon water through a sieve into a bowl. Pour in some of the lemon juice. Stir and taste. Add more juice until it tastes right.

Freezing time
1-2 hours

4 Leave the lemonade to cool in the fridge. Add the rest of the water to dilute. Stir, then pour into 18 empty yoghurt pots. Place in the freezer until partly set.

5 Push a lolly stick into each pot. Return the pots to the freezer until the lemonade becomes completely solid.

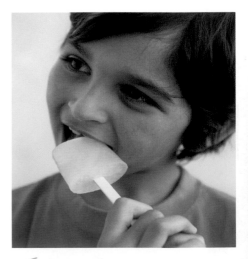

6 Crunch! Enjoy the cold juicy taste, but be quick as your lolly will quickly start to melt on a warm day.

More lemon recipes

Lemon sorbet: Scoop out a lemon and use the skin as a clever cup for lemon sorbet.

Throw in some ice cubes. Sooo cool!

For a refreshing drink, pour a little of your lemonade (from Step 3) into a glass and top up with cold fizzy water.

Herbal sun tea

Herbs have been grown all over the world for centuries for their flavour and goodness. Some herbs have been used to make healthy refreshing drinks, such as herbal teas. Using the warmth of the sun during the day, you too could make some afternoon tea from herbs you've grown or bought.

Which herbs?

Be careful to choose the right parts of each herb to make different sun teas. We used:

Jar 1: The flowers and leaves of bergamot, or bee balm.
Jar 2: The stems and leaves of epazote.
Jar 3: The leaves of mint and lemon verbena together.
Jar 4: The leaves of lemon balm and catnip together.
Jar 5: The leaves of borage.
Jar 6: The leaves of lemon grass cut into 5cm (2in) lengths.

Lemon verbena   Mint

Epazote   Bergamot

1 **Ask an adult** to drill holes in the base of an old suitcase. Place a bin liner inside and punch holes in it. Add a layer of grit and then fill the case with compost mixed with some grit.

2 **Imagine** the surface of your suitcase is a world map. Arrange the herb plants you have bought according to the position of the country they originated from.

Hold the plant by the root ball as you gently remove it from its pot.

3 **For each plant,** make a deep hole in the compost that is large enough to fit the root ball. Water the plant, then gently squeeze it out of its pot and place the plant into the hole.

4 **Fill in the soil** around the plant. The base of the stem should be level with the soil surface. Once you've planted all your herbs, water them around their roots.

Make flags to show where the herbs originally came from. For example, borage originally came from Syria and epazote from Mexico.

Make sun tea

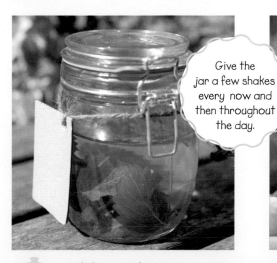

Give the jar a few shakes every now and then throughout the day.

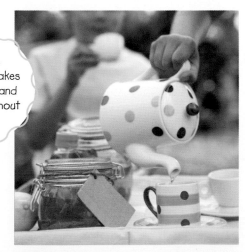

1 **In the morning,** pick 3 to 4 tablespoons of the fresh leaves, flowers, or stems depending on the herb you want to use, and put them into a jar.

2 **Add ½ a litre** (2–3 cups) of water. Put the lid of the jar on securely and give the mixture a few shakes. Leave the jar in a place that gets full sunlight.

3 **In the late afternoon,** the tea should appear a rich green in colour and be warm to drink. Strain the contents and serve. Throw away any unused tea.

Redcurrant refreshments

Like glittering rubies, redcurrants ripen on the bush from mid-summer. Add these juicy jewels to fruit salads, or squash them to make a refreshing drink like this cordial. If you can't wait for your own bush, gather these gems from a nearby pick-your-own farm.

To pick, remove the entire cluster by hand, or use scissors to cut the sprigs off.

You will need:

225g (8oz) redcurrants with stalks removed
100g (3½oz) raspberries
240g (8oz) sugar
400ml (14fl oz) cold water

1 **Ask an adult** to make a syrup by heating 240g (8oz) sugar and 400ml (14fl oz) of water slowly in a saucepan, stirring gently until the sugar has dissolved. Boil for 3 minutes, then cool.

2 **Put the fruit** into a bowl and mash it together well using the back of a fork or a potato masher. Place a damp tea towel under the bowl so it doesn't slip.

4 **Cut the end** off a clean pair of tights (make sure they're finished with) or cut a square of clean muslin, and stretch this over the top of a tall jug. Secure with an elastic band.

5 **Pour the fruit mixture** through the cloth, which will act like a fine sieve and allow only juice to pass through and collect in the bowl underneath. Leave this for an hour or two.

6 **Mix the rest** of the cooled syrup with the cordial. Pour this into a clean bottle and store it in the fridge until you need it.

A bush of your own . . .

Buy a young bush and plant it in a large container or straight into the ground. Choose a sunny open spot with a little shade. After a year or two, if you look after your plant, redcurrants will grow in abundance year after year.

In **early spring**, add a mulch of well-rotted compost to keep in the moisture and stop the weeds. Feed with a high-potash fertilizer. In **summer**, before the fruit ripens, cover the bush with a net to keep hungry birds away.

In **autumn**, once the plant is established, take cuttings to grow more bushes. Choose strong, straight stems with lots of buds, and trim into 10–15 cm (4–6 in) lengths. Push into soil in a small pot, leaving a bit above the surface. Keep them moist, and in the spring they should start to grow.

Plant your cuttings into their own pots in the following autumn. After four years, every **winter**, prune out two or three of the oldest branches.

3 **Into your mashed** fruit, pour 100ml (3½fl oz) of the sugary syrup that was prepared earlier. Stir this mixture gently, but thoroughly.

7 **When you're ready,** pour a little cordial into a jug according to taste, and add water, sparkling water, or soda water to make a refreshing treat.

Pepper hummus

Here is a recipe for red pepper hummus. And if you have any spare peppers, use them to make delicious little serving dishes.

You will need:

- 2 red peppers
- 150g (5½oz) tinned chickpeas
- 1 tsp paprika
- 1 clove garlic, peeled
- juice of ½ lemon
- 1 tbsp tahini
- 3 tbsp olive oil
- salt and pepper
- pepper shells, to serve

1 Cut each pepper into 4 and remove the stalks and seeds. Preheat the grill to high.

2 Line a grill tray with foil and place the peppers skin side up. Grill for 5 minutes or until the skins have blackened.

3 Put the hot peppers into a plastic bag and seal it up. When the peppers are cool enough to handle, peel off the blackened skins.

4 Put the peppers, chickpeas, paprika, garlic, lemon juice, tahini, and olive oil in a food processor and blend until smooth. Season to taste.

5 Spoon the hummus into pepper shells and serve.

Take out my seeds before you use me as a pot.

Potato and carrot crisps

Use home-grown potatoes and carrots to make delicious oven-baked crisps. Once you've made these, experiment with other vegetables like parsnips and beetroot.

You will need:

For the potato crisps

- 2 medium potatoes
- 2 tsp sunflower oil
- salt and pepper
- 1–2 tsp paprika (optional)

For the carrot crisps

- 2 medium carrots
- 2 tsp sunflower oil
- 2 tsp clear honey
- salt and pepper

1 **For the potato crisps,** preheat the oven to 180°C (350°F/Gas 4). Slice the potatoes using a peeler. Mix them with the oil, salt, pepper, and paprika, if using.

2 **Line a baking tray** with greaseproof paper and arrange the potato slices in a single layer. Cook for 10 minutes, turn them over, and cook for a further 10 minutes.

2 **Line a baking tray** with greaseproof paper. Arrange the carrots in a single layer and cook for 10 minutes. Turn the crisps over and cook for a further 7-10 minutes.

1 **For the carrot crisps,** preheat the oven to 180°C (350°F/Gas 4). Use a vegetable peeler to thinly slice the carrots. Mix them with the oil, honey, salt and pepper.

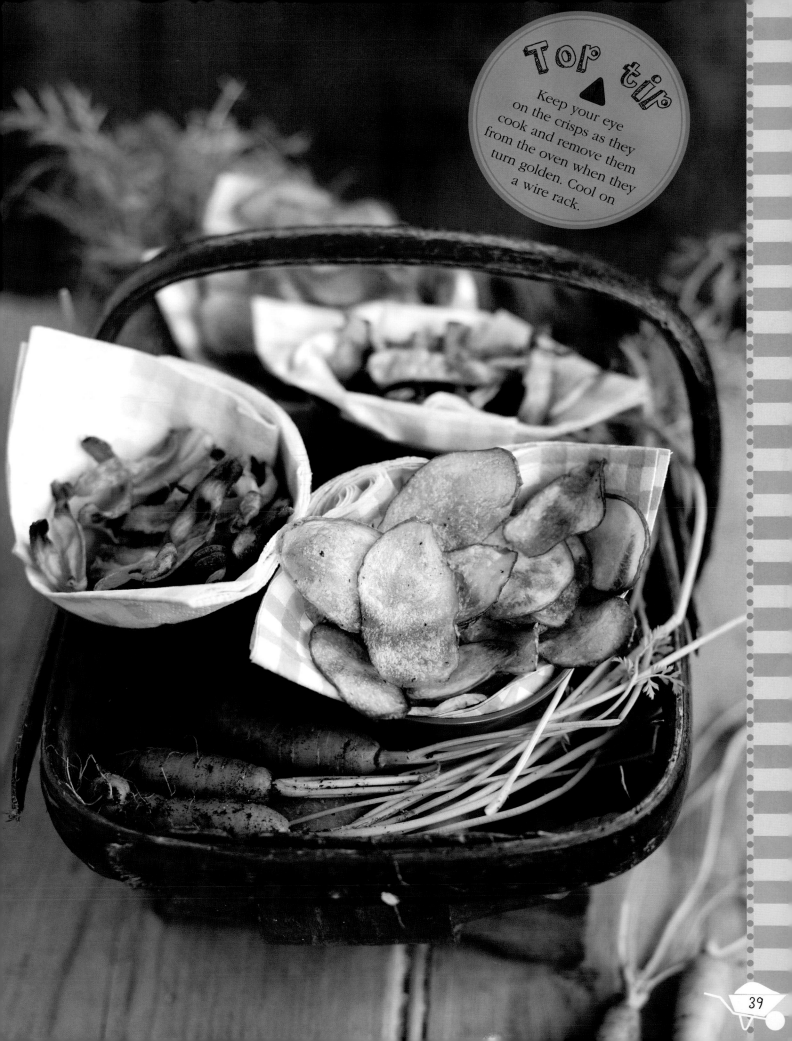

Top tip

Keep your eye on the crisps as they cook and remove them from the oven when they turn golden. Cool on a wire rack.

Blueberry cheesecake

You can grow blueberries in your garden. They taste delicious in cheesecake. Try eating them with yoghurt, or add them to muffin mixes or smoothies.

You'll need

500g (1lb) blueberries	2tbsp golden caster sugar	250g (9oz) cream cheese	200ml (7fl oz) crème fraîche	¼tsp vanilla extract	8 oat biscuits, crushed

More blueberry recipes

Try adding them to pancakes

Make yummy blueberry smoothies

They also taste great in muffins!

1 **Place ¾ of the berries** and ½ the sugar into a small saucepan. Cover and simmer for five minutes until soft. Stir in the other berries and leave to cool.

2 **Using a wooden spoon**, beat the cream cheese, crème fraîche, remaining sugar, and vanilla extract together in a mixing bowl. Continue until well mixed and soft.

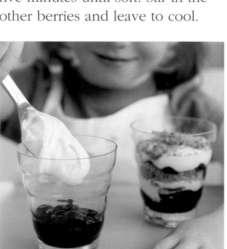

3 **Fill four glasses** with a spoonful of the blueberry sauce, then a spoonful of the cream-cheese mixture, and then a spoonful of crushed biscuits.

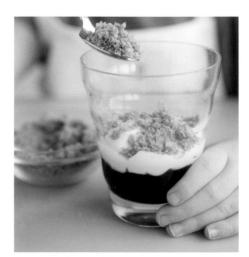

4 **Repeat the layers** once more and then put the filled glasses in the fridge for an hour.

The blueberry is one of the few fruits native to North America. Some native Americans call it a star berry because the white flowers are shaped like five-pointed stars.

Colourful kebabs

Jewel-bright skewers of garden vegetables make an ideal summer snack. Courgettes are a winner for being one of the easiest members of the squash family to grow. You can also grow peppers in your garden to use in kebabs and general cooking.

Grow in full sun and use moist, rich compost. The plants will grow to about 60 cm (2 ft) high. The seeds germinate in 1 week and the courgettes are ready to harvest in 12 weeks.

Cover the propagator with a small container that has holes poked through it to create the ideal germinating conditions.

1 **Use a propagator** to grow your seeds in. Make a 1.5 cm (½ in) deep hole, then push two seeds (on their sides) into the hole. When the seedlings appear, pull out the weakest one.

2 **Once the seedling** has grown, dig out a hole in a large prepared container. Squeeze the bottle to remove the plant. Place the plant in the hole, firm the soil around it, and water well.

3 **Add mulch** around the plant to help the soil stay moist and weed free. Make sure the mulch doesn't touch the stem.

A fungus called powdery mildew can appear on courgette plant leaves. Avoid this by keeping your plants well-watered, fed, and with space around them for good air-flow.

4 **A courgette plant** needs constantly moist soil, so bury a 15 cm (6 in) pot that has holes in its base next to the plant. Frequently water into the pot so that it will flow directly to the roots.

5 **When the first flowers** begin to form, feed the plant every 10–14 days with a tomato fertilizer and some compost tea. Do not overfeed.

6 **When the courgettes** are 10 cm (4 in) long, cut them at their base. This will encourage more courgettes to grow on your plant.

Top tip

Another good recipe is to grate courgette and mix the gratings with whisked up egg, onion, and grated cheese. Fry the mixture in a frying pan until light brown on both sides.

Create a kebab

Planning a barbecue, or need a tasty side dish? Then try out this colourful kebab.

1 **Carefully** thread some slices of yellow pepper, courgette, and baby corn and some cherry tomatoes onto some skewers or kebab sticks.

2 **Using** a pastry brush, baste the vegetables with some olive oil before placing them onto a griddle or barbecue, or under the grill. Watch them and ask an adult to turn them over a few times during cooking so that the vegetables will brown all over.

43

Create It

Fairy ring

Grow a secret fairy ring in a hidden spot at the bottom of the garden. You never know, you might attract some fairies! A circle of ornamental grasses, along with delicate sweet-smelling flowers, looks magical and makes a great place to play or have a picnic. Don't forget the fairy cakes!

You will need:

Ornamental grasses and a selection of unusually shaped flowers

Jars and glass paints or household paint and varnish

Tea lights

Walk round, dragging the stick hard into the ground to mark the edge of the circle.

1 **Make a circular** area by sticking a cane where you'd like the middle of the ring to be. Tie a long piece of string to this and tie another cane to the other end and use this to mark the edge.

2 **Use a spade** to dig out a deep trench around the edge of the circle and sprinkle some compost into the base. Put the turf that you have taken out onto a compost heap.

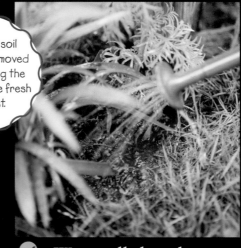

Reuse the soil that was removed when digging the trench or use fresh compost.

3 **Gently remove** each plant from its pot and place it into the trench. Fill soil around the plant's roots, pressing the soil down firmly to keep it upright.

4 **Water all the plants** well and add a decorative mulch if you wish. Continue to water the plants well during the first few weeks.

5 **Make pretty lanterns** by painting jars using special glass paint (or household paint and a layer of varnish). Place tea lights inside the jars and ask an adult to light them in the evening.

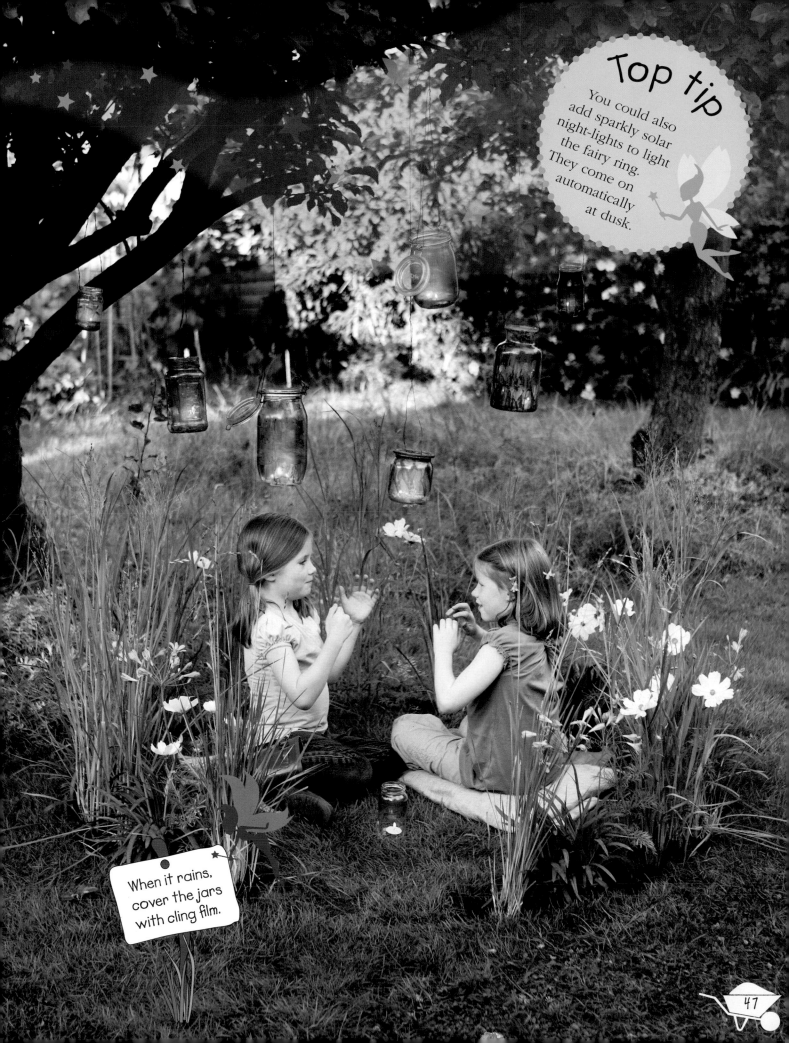

When it rains, cover the jars with cling film.

Flowerpot people

Bright, sunny sunflowers look lovely in a pot.
You can make them look even more cheerful by
painting the pot and giving them a smiley face.
For quick results, use dwarf sunflower seeds,
but if you want to grow a pot person that's taller
than you, use other varieties and a bigger pot.

Important stuff

Grow sunflowers in a place
that gets full sun.
Use well-drained soil.
Seeds will germinate
in 2-3 weeks and
flowers will open
after 7-10 weeks.

You will need:

5 litre (9 pints) tins or bigger

Enamel paints

Vaseline

Polythene bag

1 **Draw the designs** for the clothes of your flowerpot people on paper first, then use enamel paints to copy the designs onto some tins.

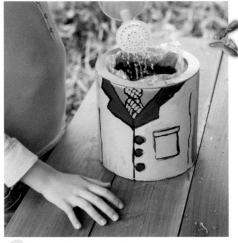

2 **Ask an adult** to make holes in the base of each tin. Then spread some gravel on the bottom for drainage. Now fill the tins up with soil and give them a good water.

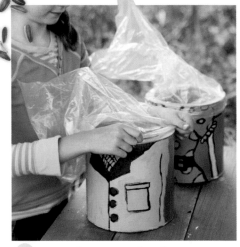

3 **Make two holes** 1.5cm (½in) deep near the centre of each pot. Sow a seed in each hole and gently cover with soil. Cover the tins with a polythene bag with a few small holes in it.

4 **Cover the sides** of the tins with a ring of vaseline to deter slugs and position in a sunny spot. Remove the bags when the seedlings' leaves appear and remove the weaker plant.

5 **Water little but often** as without water sunflowers will quickly die. If your flowers have more than one head developing, cut the extra ones later for an indoor flower display.

6 **Once the sunflowers** have opened, use a pencil or pointed stick to pick out some of the tiny flowers on the head to make a face. Eyes, noses, and mouths can be different shapes.

Pets' corner

Why not grow some tasty treats for your pets? Cats, dogs, guinea pigs, and rabbits love to nibble plants, but it's important to provide them with ones they can safely eat. The grasses grown here provide nutrition for your pets as well.

1 For the labels, cut a panel from a plastic milk carton and then draw an outline of the shape of your pet with a black marker.

2 Add features, such as whiskers, eyes, nose, and a mouth, using the black marker. Then cut out the pet shape so it's ready as a label for the container.

3 For each container, ask an adult to drill some holes in the base. Fill with a little gravel and then add compost. Moisten the compost and let the water soak through.

4 If the seeds are large, such as cat grass for cats, push them slightly below the surface and then cover them with soil using your fingertips.

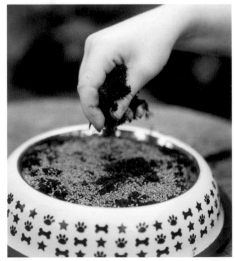

5 If the seeds are small, such as Lucerne grass for dogs, sprinkle them over the surface of the moist compost and add a thin layer of soil on top.

6 Keep the containers well watered as the plants grow. Trim the plants using scissors to keep them at a good height for your pet.

Cat grass for your cat

Lucerne grass for your dog

For other pets . . .

Sow barley, oats, and wheat for your rabbit.

Rabbit

Sow Timothy meadow grass and plantains for your guinea pigs.

Guinea pig

Plants for a fragrant garden

A garden is not just pretty to look at – if you choose the right plants, it can surround you with sweet smells all year round. The perfume comes from oils stored in the flower's petals that are released as it opens.

Roses

Flowers produce **strong scents** to attract insects and birds to pollinate them. When flowers smell nice, animals know there is pollen and nectar inside. As they land on each bloom, pollen clings to their feet and bodies and they carry it to the next flower. But not all flowers smell sweet – some have a horrible scent to attract flies.

There are some plants that only open and release their scent at night. They do this to attract night-flying pollinators, such as moths and bats.

The classic **rose** fragrance is one of the best-loved scents. There are lots of different types of rose flower. They come in a range of colours, and some have petals that are particularly thick and velvety.

Freesia

Spring flower with a powerful scent.

Jasmine

Wonderful delicately scented white blooms.

Honeysuckle

Brightly coloured, with honey-scented flowers.

Orchid

Orchids range in smell from fruity to spicy.

Fragrant flower gallery

Honeysuckle

Nicotiana

Lavender

Nicotiana blooms – also known as **flowering tobacco** – open and release their powerful fragrance when the sun goes down. Nicotiana likes moist, fertile soil and is happiest growing in partial shade. Its flowers come in reds, pinks, whites, or greens.

Honeysuckle is a strong climber that is easy to grow. The vine produces bright flowers during the summer. Plant it in the ground, then train it up a trellis.

Lavender is a classic scented flower. It is native to North Africa and the area around the Mediterranean Sea, but is now loved all over the world..

53

Lavender buddy

You can dry bunches of lavender by hanging them in a warm, dark place. After a month they'll be ready to stuff this odd little character. He's made from an old sock – but the lavender makes him smell sweet!

1 **Fill a sock** with a mixture of rice and dried lavender flowers. The rice adds weight and helps the lavender go a bit further.

2 **Twist the end** of the sock to keep the lavender and rice in place. Secure it with a few stitches.

4 **Draw arms** and legs on fabric and cut them out. For thicker limbs, fold the fabric in half and cut through both layers. Then stitch around the edges.

5 **Attach the arms** and legs securely to the body with a few firm stitches.

6 **Make curly hair** for your lavender buddy by wrapping pipe cleaners around a pencil.

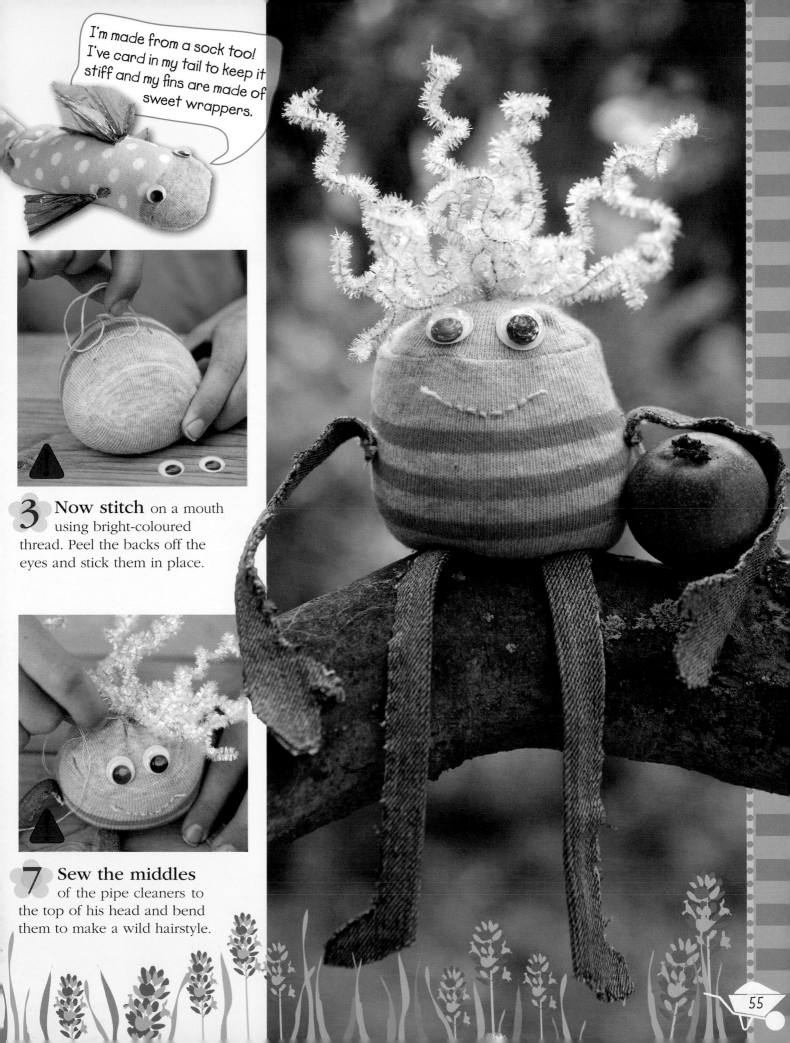

I'm made from a sock too! I've card in my tail to keep it stiff and my fins are made of sweet wrappers.

3 **Now stitch** on a mouth using bright-coloured thread. Peel the backs off the eyes and stick them in place.

7 **Sew the middles** of the pipe cleaners to the top of his head and bend them to make a wild hairstyle.

Enchanted path

Dance along your very own winding path through your garden. Make these eye-catching stepping stones by moulding concrete into pretty leafy shapes. You'll need big leaves for this project, like the ones on rhubarb, courgette, and sunflower plants.

You will need:
- disposable plastic gloves
- apron
- large plant leaves
- powdered cement mix
- large margarine container
- putty knife
- cardboard
- sand

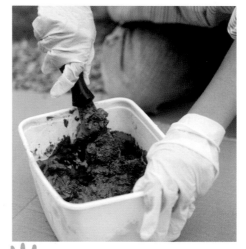

1 Mix up the cement into a thick paste in a large margarine container according to the instructions on the packaging. Remember to wear an apron and disposable plastic gloves.

2 For each stone, lay one leaf flat on a large piece of cardboard. The leaf's veiny reverse side should be facing up.

3 With a putty knife, spread the cement all over the leaf. This layer should be about 1 cm (½ in) thick at the edges, and at least 4 cm (1½ in) thick at the centre.

4 Smooth around the edges and over the surface with your putty knife, then leave your concrete leaf for about two hours, until it's just dry enough to hold its shape.

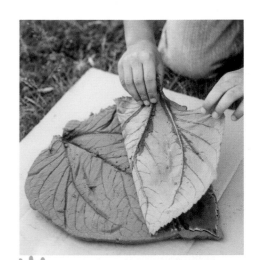

5 Gently turn it over and peel away the leaf. This will be easier if the concrete is still a bit wet. Now leave the "stone" to dry completely for a day or two.

6 **Once your stones** are really dry, decide on their position by arranging them on the grass to make sure their spacing suits your stride.

7 **Use a trowel** to mark around each shape. Remove the first stone and dig out the grass and soil to the depth of the stone plus an extra 2.5 cm (1 in).

To level the stones, add or remove sand underneath.

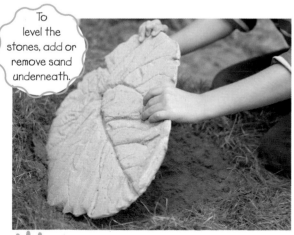

8 **Place a 2.5 cm (1 in) layer** of sand into each hole and make sure it's smooth before placing the stone on top. Repeat for all your stones, checking they're not wobbly, and filling gaps around the edge with soil.

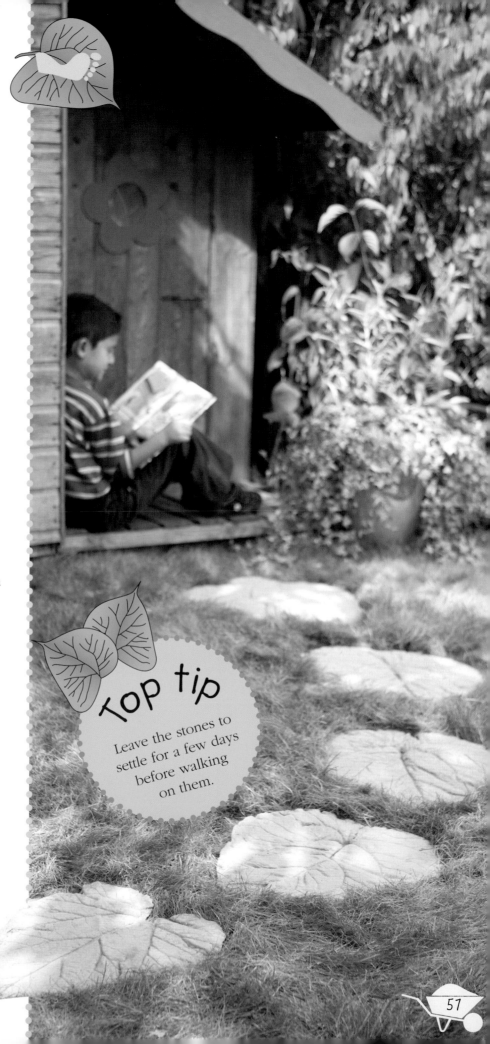

Top tip

Leave the stones to settle for a few days before walking on them.

Window box wildlife

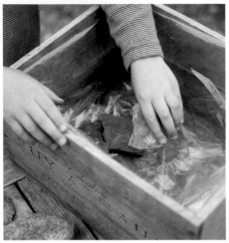

Secure your crate to a sunny window ledge.

Opening the curtains in the morning will be a whole new experience with bees, ladybirds, and butterflies flocking to your window box. Make your visitors feel at home with colourful flowers, lots of hiding places, and a nice drink of water.

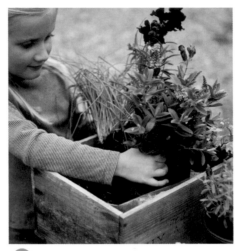

1 **If you are using** a wooden crate, put in a bin liner with some holes to prevent the wood rotting. Place rocks over the holes in the base and fill the container ¾ full of compost.

2 **First arrange** the plants, then make deep holes and place them in. Finally fill in around the plant with soil, making sure the base of the stem where it meets the root is level with the soil's surface.

3 **Water the plants** well to help them settle in. Make sure space has been left at the top of the container so that the soil won't spill over when watering or during heavy rain.

Use a flat stone to weigh the bottle down at the front end.

4 **Make a mini ladybird house** by folding some corrugated cardboard inside a bottle. Tilt the bottle downwards among the plants to prevent water getting inside.

5 **Place a small dish** or foil tray, sinking it into the soil. Fill it with water and place some small flat stones around the edge to look like a tiny pond.

6 **Tie together** some hollow sticks and dried seedpods for creatures to crawl into, and add a rock or two for them to crawl under. Once completed, place the window box on a flat surface.

We used lavender, chives, snapdragons, hebe, and ivy. These will encourage busy bees and fluttering butterflies – great pollinators. Lacewings and ladybirds will eat up pesty aphids. Many other beetles, and maybe a spider or two, could also pay you a visit.

Snapdragon

Dwarf hebe

Chives

Ivy

Lavender

Plants for a container pond

Aquatic plants are specially adapted to a watery environment and are vital ingredients for a pond. They provide oxygen, shade, shelter, and food for fish and other water creatures.

These plants provide useful resting places for dragonflies and their flowers are attractive to bees.

Emerging:
Sweet flag
(*Acorus calamus*)

Emerging:
Umbrella plant
(*Cyperus alternifolius*)

Emerging:
Duck potato
(*Sagittaria latifolia*)

Marginal:
Greater spearwort
(*Ranunculus lingua*)

Emerging plants have roots in shallow water

Giant water lilies

Giant water lilies are truly enormous! Their leaves can grow up to 3m (10ft) across. They have white flowers that open at night and give out a scent to attract beetles. At daybreak the flower closes, trapping the beetles, which become covered in pollen. The beetles are released later that evening, and move on to pollinate a new flower. The flower then turns pink.

Turn to pages 62–63 to find out how to make your own container pond at home.

These plants provide shade for the pond.

Floating plants
have leaves that float on the surface

Oxygenating: Hornwort (*Ceratophyllum demersum*)

Marginal: Bog primula (*Primula florindae*)

Marginal: Marsh marigold (*Caltha palustris*)

Floating: Frogbit (*Hydrocharis morsus-ranae*)

Floating: Water soldier (*Stratiotes aloides*)

Marginal plants
like to live in wet, boggy soil

Oxygenating plants
live underwater

Container pond

This mini pond will fit on a patio or balcony. Put it in a shady place where it won't dry out, and set it up in its final position so you don't have to drag it when it's full of water.

You will need:

- clean bricks and gravel
- large container that holds at least 40 litres (10$\frac{1}{2}$ gallons) of water
- aquatic plants
- peg basket and sacking
- fish (optional)
- rainwater

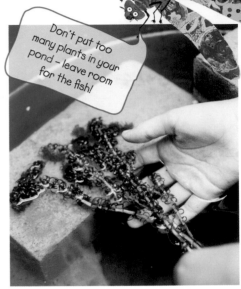

Don't put too many plants in your pond – leave room for the fish!

1 **Arrange clean bricks** in the bottom of the container to make platforms for the plants. Put clean gravel in the bottom then fill two-thirds full with rainwater.

2 **Put the oxygenating** plants, such as this hornwort, in first. Check the plant labels as some types need anchoring in the gravel, while others float freely in the water.

3 **Marginal plants**, such as sweet flag, go in next. Leave these in their pots, but put a layer of gravel on the soil to help keep it in place. Stand the pots on the bricks at the edge of the pond.

4 **You can group** marginal plants like marsh marigold and bog primula together. Line a peg basket with sacking, fill with soil, then plant your plants. Finish with a layer of gravel.

5 **Fill the container** to the top with water. Then carefully place one or two floating plants on the surface. Make sure that some of the water surface is left clear of plants.

6 **Now add your fish!** Small goldfish or mosquito fish are perfect for mini ponds. They feed on mosquito larvae and algae. Move fish to a larger container as they grow.

Put a stick in your pond as an escape route for small creatures that fall in!

Carefully add your fish to the pond so you don't injure them. Lower the bag right into the water and let the fish swim out.

Top tip

Fill or top up your pond with rainwater as tap water often has chlorine in it, which can kill fish. If you have to use tap water, let it stand for a few days so the chlorine evaporates – then add your fish.

Sweetcorn paper

The leaves that are tightly wrapped around sweetcorn are called the husk. You can flatten these and paste them together to make paper. It takes about two weeks to dry, then you can use it to make beautiful gifts.

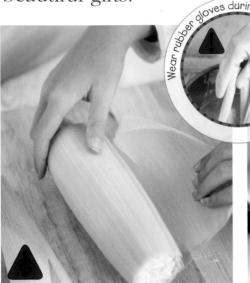

Wear rubber gloves during steps 2 and 3.

1 **Cut the top** and bottom off the sweetcorn cob and carefully peel off the husk. Try to keep each leaf in one piece. Make sure you have an adult helping you.

2 **Fill a large pan** with water and stir in one tbsp washing soda for every litre (1.7 pints) of water. Add the husks, bring to the boil, and simmer for about 30 minutes.

3 **Rinse the leaves** in plenty of cold water and leave them to drain on kitchen paper or an old tea towel. Pat them as dry as possible with kitchen paper.

To make flour paste, mix together 1 tsp flour and 2 tsp water.

The finished paper

4 **Arrange the leaves** in a row so the edges overlap slightly. Stick the edges together with flour paste.

5 **Spread the leaves** with paste, then put another layer on top at 90 degrees to the first. This is one sheet of paper.

6 **Sandwich** your paper between tea towels, then newspaper. Weight down with something heavy. Replace the newspaper when wet.

Gifts
Paint someone special a mini masterpiece on the paper you've made. You will need a frame and some acrylic paints and brushes.

Make a gift tag

Make a notebook
Cover a notebook with brown cardboard and stick a piece of sweetcorn paper on top. Then paint a picture to decorate it.

Make a hole with a pen and thread some ribbon through each cover to finish the book.

Wild-West cacti

Yee-hah! Turn a container into a desert landscape by filling it with prickly cacti and other succulents. Because they store water in their fleshy leaves, stems, or roots, succulents can survive in harsh conditions such as deserts, scrublands, and mountains.

Horticultural sand   Perlite   Peat-based compost

Most cacti and succulents need soil that lets water drain away quickly to stop the plants from rotting. So use either a cactus potting mix, or create your own using equal amounts of peat-based compost and coarse sand. Add some perlite or vermiculite as these also allow for quick draining.

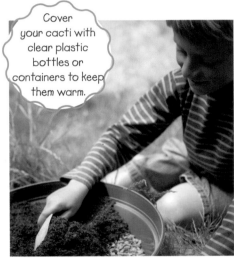

Cover your cacti with clear plastic bottles or containers to keep them warm.

1 **Sprinkle a thin layer** of gravel into a seed tray. Most cacti have shallow roots since they store water in their stems. Add 2–5cm (1–2in) of cactus potting mix, and make holes for the plants.

2 **Beginning with the** largest cactus, ease each plant gently out of its old container. To do this, wear gloves and use tongs or wrap the cactus in newspaper, paper towels, or light cardboard.

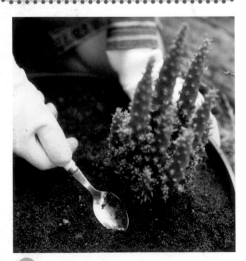

3 **Place the first cactus** into its hole and use the back of a spoon to press the soil down around its base. Transplant the rest of the plants in the same way.

4 **Mist the soil or** sprinkle it lightly with lukewarm water. Repeat after the potting mix has looked very dry for a few days.

5 **Add details to make** your landscape look like the Wild West. Create a track using sand or gravel, for example, and add model cowboys and injuns.

Place your landscape in a warm, partly shaded site.

This is a hairy trumpet cactus.

Plants for topiary

Topiary is the centuries-old art of clipping trees and shrubs into decorative shapes. It's also a way of training climbing plants around a frame. The result is anything from a neat pom-pom to an elephant.

Making shapes

Use a small-leaved, evergreen plant. Since the leaves remain all year, so does your shape! You'll also need a wire frame to grow plants around or to use as a guide to cutting. Buy or make your frame.

A wire frame can be simple, like a heart, or more complicated, like this seahorse. Wrap the plant around the frame as it grows. Snip off any shoots growing in the wrong direction.

For clipped topiary, put your frame over the plant. Snip the plant to the shape of the frame.

Trim little and often as your plant takes shape.

Cone

Chicken

Pom-pom

Privet

Traditionally used for garden hedges.

Yew

A dense, slow-growing evergreen.

Box

Good for small topiary.

Shrubby honeysuckle

A fast-growing hedging plant.

Juniper

A hardy plant with dense leaves.

Choose a healthy plant with an even shape

Plant watch

When you snip your plant, keep the cuts neat – ragged edges look untidy. Ideally trim in early summer. Never trim when there is a frost as this can damage the plant.

Topiarists trim their creations using scissors, secateurs, or hand shears. Electric hedge trimmers can also be used for large creations.

Topiary shears

Elephant and rider

Spiral topiary

Ivy man

If you don't want to wait for years for a topiary figure to take shape, try your hand at this ivy man. He's made from a wire frame and will spring to life in just a few months.

You will need:

- garden wire
- scissors or wire cutters
- window box or similar container
- general-purpose compost
- small stick
- metal food tray
- two small-leaved ivy plants

1 **For the head,** ask an adult to help you twist a length of wire into an oval, leaving enough wire to make the neck. Make sure your ivy man is the right size to fit the container.

2 **Take another** length of wire and make a second oval, twisting it around the first to make a 3-D head. Secure it at the neck.

4 **Fill a container** with general-purpose compost. Position your ivy man. To help him stand up, try making a spade from a stick and metal food tray. Plant the ivy.

5 **Plant ivy** at the base of each leg and wrap the tendrils around the frame.

Plant watch

Ivy is a climbing plant that loves to scramble up walls, trees, and fences. It can reach as high as 30 m (100 ft) above the ground. Ivy hauls itself up using aerial roots that grow along its stem. These help the plant to grip the surface.

3 **Make the body** by
twisting more wire into a
body shape. Include spikes to anchor
the frame in the ground. Attach the
body to the head and wrap more
wire around the whole thing.

6 **As the ivy grows,** thread
it through the frame. Clip out
any shoots that are growing in the
wrong direction. After a few months,
ivy will cover the whole frame.

Insect-eating plant

Sundews like to live in a sunny spot.

Keep well watered. Sundews only drink soft water or rain water.

Some sundews can live for up to 50 years.

Here's a mini world in a jar, and the plant at the centre is an insect-eating sundew. Sit it on a sunny windowsill and sticky droplets form on its leaves. Passing insects stick to these and are digested to death. Team up the sundew with plasticine aliens to make a bottle garden that's out of this world!

You will need:

- aquarium gravel or recycled beads and stones
- large plastic storage jar
- glitter
- carnivorous plant compost
- sundew carnivorous plant
- plasticine

1 Start by dropping coloured gravel into the bottom of your storage jar. Make layers using different colours and sprinkle on glitter for sparkle.

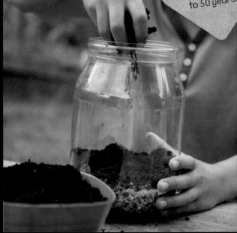

2 Now drop in handfuls of compost. Press it down gently. Make sure you leave enough room for the sundew!

4 Make your alien. No one knows what an alien looks like, so they can be any shape you like! Squash some plasticine into a body and add eyes, arms, and legs.

5 Here's one we made earlier. Think about where your alien will go. Inside the jar? Sticking to the outside? This will help you decide how big to make it.

Look out alien dragonfly – there's a sticky trap below!

Plant watch

Sundews are also called Drosera. There are more than 160 types. They attract insects using their bright colours and the sweet droplets that cover their leaves. Once an insect is stuck, some Drosera curl their leaves around it as it dies.

3 **Remove the sundew** from its pot, plant it in the middle of the compost, and firm the compost gently around it.

Small fly

6 **Leave your alien** world to settle. The sundew will start to form new droplets on its leaves that small flies will stick to.

Top tip

Carnivorous plants usually like a peat and sand mix of compost. You can buy it ready mixed, or make your own using two parts moss peat to one part sand.

73

Bug quiz

Are insects the only bugs?

The word "bugs" can include not just insects, but also other creepy crawlies that have no backbones, such as scorpions, millipedes, and woodlice.

5 FACTS ABOUT BUTTERFLIES

- There are 20,000 different species all over the world.
- We eat flower nectar (a sweet liquid) and pollen (a fine powder).
- Most of us live in tropical rainforests.
- We are very light.
- We are eaten by birds.

Why don't spiders get stuck in their own webs?

Only some of the silky strands on spider webs are sticky for catching insects. Spiders don't step on these. We may also use some of our tiny claws on our feet to lift the sticky strands out of the way.

5 FACTS ABOUT BUGS

- There are well over a million species around the world.
- The largest group of bugs are insects.
- Many bugs eat plants, some eat other insects, and others eat blood, dung, or decaying things.
- Some of us can bite and sting, while others can pinch with their mouthparts.
- We shed our skin (moult) as we grow, sometimes completely transforming for out last adult stage.

Why are butterflies so colourful?

Colourful wings are very important to us. Our colours help us to hide ourselves or startle enemies. They help us to keep us warm and to attract a mate.

5 FACTS ABOUT SPIDERS

- There are 40,000 species of spiders.
- Most of us live on our own.
- Most species live for 1-2 years, but tarantulas can live much longer.
- Different species eat different things.
- Female spiders lay more than 1,000 eggs at a time and wrap them in a silk egg sac.

5 FACTS ABOUT ANTS

- There are about 35,000 species of ants.

- We are found all over the world, except Antarctica.

- Our nests can be found in trees, just below the earth, or deep underground.

- Just the queen ant lays eggs.

- One of our main enemies is other ants.

Do all bees make honey?

Very few bees make honey and only honeybees store enough for you to take some, too. I am a bumblebee and I only make about 3ml (½ teaspoon) of honey in my lifetime.

5 FACTS ABOUT BEES

- There are about 2,000 species of bees around the world.

- We feed on pollen and nectar.

- We help plants to make fruit by pollinating them.

- Our young are called larvae.

- We have many enemies, such as frogs, toads, and insect-eating birds plus bugs including wasps and spiders.

Why do ants have armies?

We are social insects, which means we live in a group, or colony, to help us survive. We each have jobs to do. Most of us are workers but some are soldiers, guarding the nest. Soldier ants defend the colony by biting, stinging, or spraying acid on attackers.

5 FACTS ABOUT DRAGONFLIES

- There are more than 5,000 different species.

- We can be found on every continent except Antarctica.

- We eat other bugs, such as mosquitoes, midges, and spiders.

- We have been round for 300 million years.

- We do not harm people.

Are all ladybirds spotty?

Most ladybirds are spotted but not all of us. The ladybirds with the most spots have 24. But there are a few of us who have white stripes instead of black spots, and some of us have no markings at all.

Why are all dragonflies in a hurry?

We don't have very long to live as adults, so we zoom around finding food and a mate. The largest dragonflies can fly up to 40–60 km/h (25–38 mph), making us the fastest flying insects.

5 FACTS ABOUT LADYBIRDS

- There are over 5,000 species all over the world.

- We are beetles.

- We live in trees, shrubs, fields, beaches, and even in your home.

- We eat garden pests, such as aphids, mealybugs, and mites.

- Most of us don't bite.

Cool plants to grow

Get ready to impress your friends with some unusual plants, from ones that look, smell, or feel strange to those with surprising behaviour. Some can be grown from seed or bought from shops, while others can be started in some unusual ways.

1

Tickle-me plant *Mimosa pudica*

Germinates in 2-3 weeks | 30 cm (12 in)

When touched, the fern-like leaves of this very sensitive plant curl up, setting off a chain reaction where nearby leaf stalks of the plant fold in, too. The leaves also fold over in the dark. If touched too many times, the plant's reaction may slow down.

2

Coleus *Coleus blumei*

Germinates in 2 weeks | Dwarf and tall varieties

Grown indoors or outdoors, this eye-catching plant has dramatic, colourful leaves. Encourage the plant to become bushy and last longer by pinching out the small flowers and growing shoots at the end of summer.

3

Avocado stone *Persea americana*

Germinates in 6 weeks | Very tall tree

Impress yourself as well as your friends by growing your own avocado plant from its stone. Push three toothpicks into the centre of the stone (pointy end upwards), and place over a jar full of water so that the stone dips in. A seedling will form.

6

Ornamental gourds *Curcurbita pepo*

Germinates in 2 weeks | Height varies

There's an impressive array of strangely shaped, coloured, and patterned gourds to choose from. In the autumn, they can be dried to make interesting hanging decorations or the larger gourds can be hollowed out to become interesting plant containers.

7

Pineapple top *Ananas comosus*

Rooting: in 6-8 weeks | 30 cm (12 in)

Slice the leafy top off a fresh pineapple, strip away a few leaves at the base, leave to dry, and then place into a pot with compost and keep moist. Hey presto – within six weeks the top starts to root! Although it will be a year or two before it fruits.

8

Chocolate cosmos *Cosmos atrosanguineus*

Germinates in 5-10 days | 90 cm (3 ft)

The dark brown-red flowers of this perennial plant produce a powerful smell of vanilla and sweet chocolate. Originally from Mexico, the plant is no longer found in the wild. The blooms last through the summer and into the autumn.

4

Lablab beans *Lablab purpureus*

Germinates in 2-3 weeks | 2m (6 ft)

Lablab beans are climbing plants that produce pods that can be eaten when cooked. They have stunning purple and pink fragrant flowers followed by fascinating dark purple seedpods, surrounded by green and purple-brown leaves.

5

Maize (corn) *Zea mays*

Germinates in 1-2 weeks | 1.5 m (5 ft)

Sow some maize seeds bought from a pet shop into a container about 10 cm (4 in) apart and, if kept moist, fertilized, and warm, in about 3 months corncobs will be ready to harvest. It's a-maize-ing!

9

Venus flytrap *Dionaea muscipula*

Germinates in 4-6 weeks | 15 cm (6 in)

Venus flytraps survive by feeding on flies and other insects. They are fascinating to watch for their reactions. You could feed your plant, using tweezers to place an insect inside its head-trap every ten days. Avoid touching the trigger hairs.

10

Lemon verbena *Alpysia triphylla*

Germinates in 2-3 weeks | A bushy shrub

If you rub your fingers on the leaves of the lemon verbena plant, they will pick up a powerful smell of lemon. On page 33, we've used these leaves to flavour herbal teas. They can also be added to potpourris. New plants can be grown by taking cuttings.

Glossary

Annual
A plant that completes its whole life cycle in a year.

Aquatic plant
A plant whose roots are permanently under water. The rest of the plant may also be fully submerged or float on the surface.

Cactus
A spiny plant that can store water inside its stem.

Carnivorous plant
A plant that captures and eats insects to obtain nutrients that it cannot get from the soil.

Compost
Potting compost is a special soil mix for growing plants in pots. Garden compost is a soil improver made from decayed plants.

Fertilizer
A mixture that encourages plants to grow.

Flower
This is the structure that contains the male and female parts of the plant.

Fruit
The part of a plant that forms when a flower is pollinated. The fleshy part protects the seeds inside.

Germination
When seeds sprout and start to grow.

Grasses
A family of flowering plants that have narrow leaves growing from the base. They include the cereal crops, such as wheat and barley.

Green gardening
A way of gardening that is environmentally friendly, encouraging wildlife and using homemade compost rather than artificial chemicals.

Leaf
The part of a plant that makes the plant's food. This is a process called photosynthesis. A leaf takes in carbon dioxide from the air and uses sunlight to join this with water to make sugar-based food.

Moist
Slightly wet.

Mulch
A thick layer covering the surface of the soil that keeps in the moisture, prevents weeds growing, and helps to protect the roots from cold. Some add nutrients to the soil.

Pests
Any bug or animal in the garden that harms plants.

Pesticide
A chemical that is used to kill insects, slugs, snails, and other small creatures that damage plants.

Pollination
The process of transferring pollen from the male part of a flower to the female part so that seeds can be produced.

Roots
The underground parts of a plant that take up minerals and water from the soil and support the plant. Enlarged roots, such as carrots, store food and water.

Seed
A part of a flowering plant that contains a baby plant and a store of food to get it started.

Sprout
A seed that has just begun to germinate.

Topiary
Cutting trees and shrubs so that they grow into interesting shapes.

Transplant
To move a young plant that has outgrown its pot into a larger container.

Vegetable
The edible leaf, stem, or root of a plant. Some plants that are commonly called vegetables, such as peppers and tomatoes, are actually fruits.

Index

Acknowledgements

Dorling Kindersley would like to thank:

**Photographer
Will Heap
www.willheap.com**

• Vauxhall City Farm for use of their allotments for additional photography. Dianne Sullock, Sharon Clouston and Bernadette Kennedy from Vauxhall City Farm.

• Capel Manor College for the use of their garden and for taking care of our plants. The Capel Manor Team: Tony Monaghan, Sarah Neophytou, and Joanna Bates

• Brockwell Community Greenhouses for the use of their area, and especially to Fabrice Boltho and Dianne Sullock, the site supervisers, for helping us to arrange location usage

• Steiner Hoathly Hill Community in West Sussex for use of their grounds

• Antonia Salt at Green Ink

• Brockwell Community Greenhouses

• Roots and Shoots,

• Alleyn Park Garden Centre Ltd.

• Garsons Farm Shop

• The Garlic Farm

• Defland Nurseries Ltd.

• Keift & Sons Ltd. for supplies

• Annie Nichols for food styling

• Kate Heap for props and styling

• Secret Seed Society for providing all the plant characters in this book

• RAGT Seeds for supplying wheat products

• Meredith Mistry for making sweet-smelling lavender buddies

• David Crawford for making sweetcorn paper

• Jim Arbury, RHS Wisley, for supplying loofah plants

• The staff at Shoots Garden Centre, Stanmore, Middlesex, for plants and advice.

• David Arnold, Sutton Seeds, for supplying tomato, sweetcorn, and pepper plants.

• Jon Wheatley and Mary Payne MBE, horticultural consultant, Stonebarn Landscapes Limited, for supplying vegetable plants.

• Hannah and Molly for illustrating the sweetcorn paper and notebooks on page 65

• Our models: Cherry, Camron, Molly, Sophia, Zeynep, Christian, Solly, Omid Alavi, Rhianna Bryan, Cara Crosby-Irons, Scarlet and Stanley Heap, Fiona Lock, Kieran and Jane Mistry, Hannah and Max Moore, Matthew Morley, Jamie Chang-Leng, Spencer Britton, Kitty Nallet, Saphira Noor, Julia Scott, Alfred and Molly Warren

Picture credits

**All images © Dorling Kindersley
For further information see: www.dkimages.com**

Thank you everyone!

Our models

Here are some of the lovely models who took part in the photos.

Cherry Camron Sophia Zeynep Christian Hannah Solly

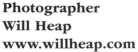